25 STORIES FOR CHILDREN

AND ALSO FOR TEENS

J.P. Vaswani

Credit page

Published by:
Gita Publishing House
Sadhu Vaswani Mission,
10, Sadhu Vaswani Path,
Pune 411 001, (India).
gph@sadhuvaswani.org
www.dadavaswanisbooks.org

Second Edition

ISBN: 978-93-80743-08-0

Printed by:
Mehta Offset Pvt. Ltd.
Mehta House,
A-16, Naraina Industrial Area II, New Delhi 110 028, (India).
info@mehtaoffset.com

WHY BEG FROM A BEGGAR

A sanyasin was in need of some help for an orphanage he was running. He came to see the king of the realm and was told that he was in his prayer-room,offering worship to God.

Quickly, the sanyasin came and stood outside the door of the room.He heard the king pray, "So bless me,Lord, that my years on earth may multiply, my wealth may increase, the borders of my realm may widen evermore....!"

Hearing this prayer, the sanyasin turned to go. And when they asked him, "O holy man! Why are you going away without meeting the king?" he answered. "I did not know, I was coming to beg from one who is himself a beggar! From today I shall beg of Him at whose door even kings stand as beggars!"

"YOU ARE ALREADY FIVE YEARS LATE"

Aristotle was the most respected teacher in Athens. The city's best and brightest young men gathered around him at his Lyceum to receive an all-round 'liberal' education,aimed at making them ideal citizens and ideal human beings.

Once, a young mother approached Aristotle. She dreamt of the day when her little son would become Aristotle's student. In her eagerness she wanted the boy to be prepared for it right from his childhood.

"When should I begin training my child, so that he may grow up to be an ideal human being?" she asked the great teacher.

"How old is your child?" enquired Aristotle.

"He is barely five now, " said the eager mother.

"Waste no more time, dear lady," said Aristotle. "You are already five years late."

Aristotle was Greek Philospher and Teacher.He was pupil of Plato and tutor of Alexander the Great.

THE EMPEROR AND THE SOLDIER

Alexander the Great was leading his army across continents. Wherever he marched, victory greeted him. Thrones trembled at his approach. Kings and princes bowed down before his power and military might.

One dark, wintry night, Alexander's army reached a remote village after a long march. It was snowing. The cold seemed to freeze the very marrow of their bones.

Alighting from his horse, the Emperor ordered his servants to light a fire forthwith. As his tent was being put up, a reclining seat was placed before the fire so that he could warm himself in comfort.

As he held out his benumbed fingers to catch the warmth of the roaring fire, Alexander's eyes fell on an old soldier, standing at a distance. He was shivering in the bitter cold, his teeth chattered, and his arms and legs seemed to tremble.

Quietly Alexander left the fireside and walked up to the old soldier. Gently but firmly, he led the soldier to his chair. "Sit down and warm yourself, my comrade-in-arms", he said.

Of such stuff are great Emperors made.

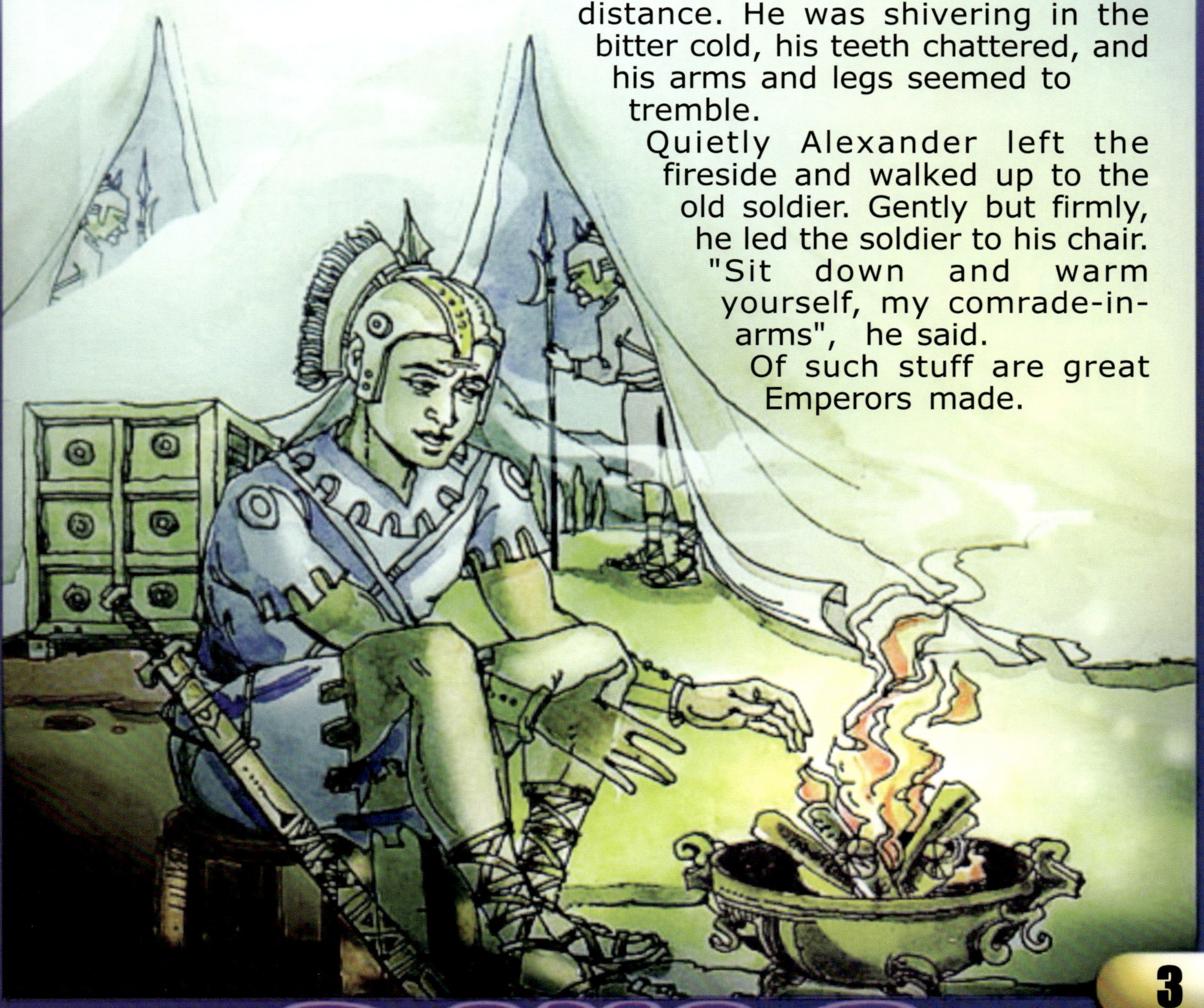

THE TREMENDOUS POWER OF ATTITUDE

Psychologists have always told us that attitudes can influence results. Two scientists decided to conduct an experiment to find out if attitudes could affect seeds. Two identical cans were taken. Into each was poured soil and fertilizer of the same quality and quantity, and 23 seeds were dropped into each can. They were both placed in a greenhouse so that they could have the same conditions of weather and temperature.

There was only one variable in the experiment, all other things being the same. Everyday, the two scientists came to the greenhouse, and standing before the first can poured into it all the negativism of which they were capable. They said to the seeds, "You are good for nothing. Nothing is ever going to come

out of you and even if something comes out, it is not going to last", and so on and so forth.
Then they came and stood in front of the second can and poured into it all the positivism of which they were capable.
"You are so wonderful," they said to the seeds, "and you are going to show wonderful results. It will be a sight to see what is coming out of you", and so on and so forth.
This was repeated thrice a day for three weeks.
At the end of the three weeks, the scientists found that while there came forth only two or three shoots of grass out of the first can,out of the second can, there came forth whole strands of grass, so strong that they could clutch it and lift up the entire can with its soil and fertilizer. If this is what attitude can do to seeds what can it not do to human beings?

LOOKING FOR MY FRIEND

Malik was a holy man. He was loved and respected by all his neighbours as a man of God. A young man who lived in the neighbourhood, was notorious for his profligacy and bad behaviour. He was a constant source of chagrin to all the people who lived in the locality. They appealed to Malik to have a word with him. Perhaps, the holy man's counsel would help him change his ways, they felt.Malik went to meet the young man. Gently, he urged him to mend his behaviour.

"I'm a protégé of the Sultan!" replied the youth arrogantly. "I can do whatever I like, and no one dare question me."

"What if the people complain to the Sultan about you?" asked Malik.

"That will be quite useless," laughed the youth. "The Sultan

is so fond of me that he will not hear a word against me!"
"I shall complain to the Sultan of Sultans to- Allah Himself," warned Malik."0, He is All-Beneficent, All-Merciful! He is too forgiving to condemn me!" replied the youth nonchalantly.His behaviour grew from bad to worse.Finding it impossible to tolerate his ways, the entire neighbourhood decided to confront him and protest against his profligacy. Malik agreed to join them.That night, Malik had a dream in which a Voice urged him, "Do not reproach My friend. He is under My protection."When Malik awoke the next morning, he clearly remembered the words. He did not join the neighbours who berated the youth severely.
The young man was surprised that Malik was not among them. Later that day, he came to Malik and asked him, "Why weren't you with the rest? " Malik narrated his dream to the young man. He repeated what the Voice had said to him, "Do not reproach My friend, for he is under My protection. "The profligate was stunned. "Did He really call me His friend?" he demanded."That was what He said to me," Malik asserted.The young man was not seen in the locality any more. People wondered what had happened to him. He had not seemed to take their warnings seriously. Where could he have gone?Years rolled by. On a pilgrimage to Mecca, Malik met the young man. Surprised by his presence at the holy city, he asked the youth, "What brings you here?"
"Ever since the day that you told me about Him, I have been here, searching for my Friend,"the youth replied. "I shall continue to look for Him until I find Him!"

KIDNAPPED!

Sadhu Vaswani was just three or four years old at that time. One sultry afternoon, he stood outside his house, gazing at the few passers-by.

It was the afternoon siesta hour. People were dozing comfortably in the cool interior of their houses, and the whole area wore a deserted look. Suddenly, a fierce looking, huge pathan appeared before the child. Before he could realize what was happening, the child felt a rough hand catch hold of him by the scruff of his neck and he was thrust into a pit of darkness!

It took the child a long minute to realize what was happening. He was being spirited away, hidden in the pathan's flowing salwar!
"Help me God, Oh help me!" he prayed fervently. "Save me from this darkness!"
A few passers-by began to eye suspiciously, the awkward movement of the pathan and the mysterious movement in his flowing garment, as the child continued to struggle.
Realizing that he was being watched, the pathan stopped near a doorway. Adroitly pulling the child out of his hiding, he put him on the doorstep and vanished as suddenly as he had appeared.
Referring to this incident,Sadhu Vaswani said later, "We are in the darkness of avidya- ignorance. We need to offer, again and again, the prayer of the ancient Rishi. Tamaso ma jyotir gamaya- O Lord, out of darkness, lead me into light!"

THREE SECRETS OF SUCCESS

A hunter cought a beautiful rare bird in his net, dilated with his catch, he locked it out in a cage,when suddenly the bird spoke to him. "O hunter!" it said in a sweet and melodious voice, "I am such a tiny bird, that you will get nothing out of me.If you sell me, I shall fetch you but little.If you kill me and eat me,you will only get a tiny piece of flesh.But if you release me, set me free from the cage,I shall pass on to you three secrets of success. If you follow them you are sure to be rich prosperous and successful."

Intrigued, the hunter let the bird out of the cage.It flew up to the branch of a tree and promptly uttered its promised secrets, "The first secret is this-never, never, never accept anything that goes against

your common sense. The second-never, never, cry over spilt milk. And the third-never ever attempt that which is impossible!"

The hunter was very annoyed.

"What a silly bird you are!" he cried. "I should not have released you. You are nothing but a worthless creature!"

"Worthless? Me?" cried the bird. "Why, if you cut my heart open, you will find a diamond larger than the famed kohinoor!"

The hunter was beside himself with greed. He jumped up and scrambled all over the branches of the tree, as the little bird flew higher. There was no way he could catch the bird, and eventually he fell down, bruised all over, with one leg broken!

"Let me repeat those three rules of success to you," said the bird from the top of the tree. "I told you never to believe anything that goes against your common sense. Whoever has heard of a bird with a diamond in its heart? You did not follow the first rule!

"Never cry over spilt milk-was the second rule I gave you. You let me out of the cage and you regretted it later. What a wasteful gesture!"

"The third rule, O hunter-never attempt the impossible. Look at you now! You tried to catch a bird on a tree-and ended up with a broken leg!"

"My time is up, and I must fly away," concluded the bird. "But truly, you failed to benefit from the secrets of success that I taught you!"

THE WISDOM OF A POOR WOMAN

After the Russian Revolution, atheism became a powerful movement all over the Republic of the Soviet Union. Atheists set about to destroy all places of worship-temples, churches and mosques were systematically pulled down.

Flushed with the success of their 'achievement', the atheists crowed, "Where is God?"

In a remote village in Russia, an atheist came upon a poor, old woman turning the beads of her rosary in pious worship.

"Throw away your rosary, you foolish woman!" he thundered. "There is no God to hear your prayers."

The old woman calmly gazed into his eyes.

"You may say what you please, brother!" she said gently. "But everything in this world bears witness to His existence."

"You may close down temples, churches and mosques, but you cannot extinguish the stars. Every star bears witness to the truth that God is."

AN ELEPHANT AMONGST MEN

There is a beautiful, touching story concerning the Buddha. He had grown in years and in influence. He was followed by devoted crowds wherever he went. Thousands upon thousands-many of them rich noblemen, who had renounced their riches and their lives of comfort and ease-had joined his Order and become wandering *bhikkhus,* cheerfully accepting the rigours of a homeless life.

Devadatta was a cousin and disciple of the Master. Infatuated with the lust for power, Devadatta wished to set himself up as the leader of the Order. But this would not happen so long as the Buddha continued to live. Devadatta secretly plotted to put an end to the Buddha's life.

Nalagiri was a fierce wild elephant, belonging to King Ajatasatru. The elephant was always kept in chains. Devadatta so arranged that when the Buddha passed by, Nalagiri would be let loose after him.

As was his custom, the Buddha, with several of the *bhikkhus,* passed along the road early in the morning. Nalagiri was let loose. Raising a

veritable dust-storm, the manslayer charged after the band of docile *bhikkhus.* They were terrified, they scattered in all directions, fleeing from the enraged tusker. Alas! In the face of danger, they, like so many of us, forgot their oft-repeated vow, *"Buddham sharanam gachhami!* I seek refuge in the Buddha!"

Only a faithful few remained with the Master. They, too, were terrified but like true disciples, they considered their own life as of insignificant value compared to that of the Master. And they pleaded with him to run to some place of safety. Calm was the face of the Buddha, serene were his eyes, lit up as ever with the light of compassion. And to his disciples he said, "Fear not my brethren! He who harmeth none, will be harmed by no one!"

There was panic all along the roads. People clambered onto the roofs of houses on both the sides of the road. Death was abroad. The people felt intensely for the Buddha and the small number of bhikkhus who would not leave their beloved Master even in this moment of impending doom. From the roof tops the people gazed at the Buddha and exclaimed, "What loveliness in his face! What light! What beauty! Yet will the elephant not spare even the Blessed One!" And there were some who declared, "What harm can this elephant, Nalagiri, do to him who is an elephant among men?"

The atmosphere was charged with tension and apprehension. The Buddha was calm. And with infinite compassion in his lotus-eyes, he looked at the steadily advancing elephant, which was almost upon him. An agonised cry went forth from the housetops, "May the Blessed One be safe from harm!"

Call it a miracle, if you will! It was not a miracle, it was the magic of the Master's presence, of one who would harm no one in thought, word or deed! The elephant bowed down to the Master, then quietly got up! The Master stroked his forehead and spoke a gentle word or two of love. Nalagiri had become a new elephant, tame and docile. Overwhelmed with joy and relief, they cried out, "Wild elephants are tamed with buffets and blows. But the great elephant among men has tamed Nalagiri with a blessing and a smile!"

THE UNSTRUNG BOW

A little known incident from the life of Aesop reveals a totally new dimension to the great story-teller whose fables are world-renowned.

One day, Aesop was playing with little children, shouting and dancing and laughing with them.

An Athenian passed by; he expressed surprise that a mature adult should waste his time thus.

In answer, Aesop picked up a bow and unstringing it, laid it on the ground. To the Athenian, he said, "O wise one! Tell me the meaning of this unstrung bow!"

The man was perplexed. He said, "Tell me what it means."
And Aesop said to him, "If you keep a bow always bent, it will lose its elasticity. But if you let it go slack, it will be fitter for use when you need it."
Are we not, many of us, like the bent bow, always highly strung? We need to unstring ourselves, to relax, from time to time, that we may be "fitter for use" when we are called to action. And to relax, we need to learn to "let go".

THE STORY OF DHRUVA

Child Dhruva was the eldest son of his father, who was a king. As the eldest, he should have been the closest to his father's heart, he should have been the crown prince and heir to the throne. But the child was meant for a greater life!

Dhruva's father had two wives-Suniti, the older one, was gentle, mild and virtuous. She was Dhruva's mother. Suruchi, the younger one, was beautiful, and the king's favourite. She had a son called Uttama.

One day, the two princes were playing together. Suddenly, Dhruva wanted to go and sit on the lap of his father, the king. The little boy ran up to his father who was seated on the throne, and climbed joyfully onto his knees. The king, too, embraced his little son gladly, and lovingly stroked his hair.

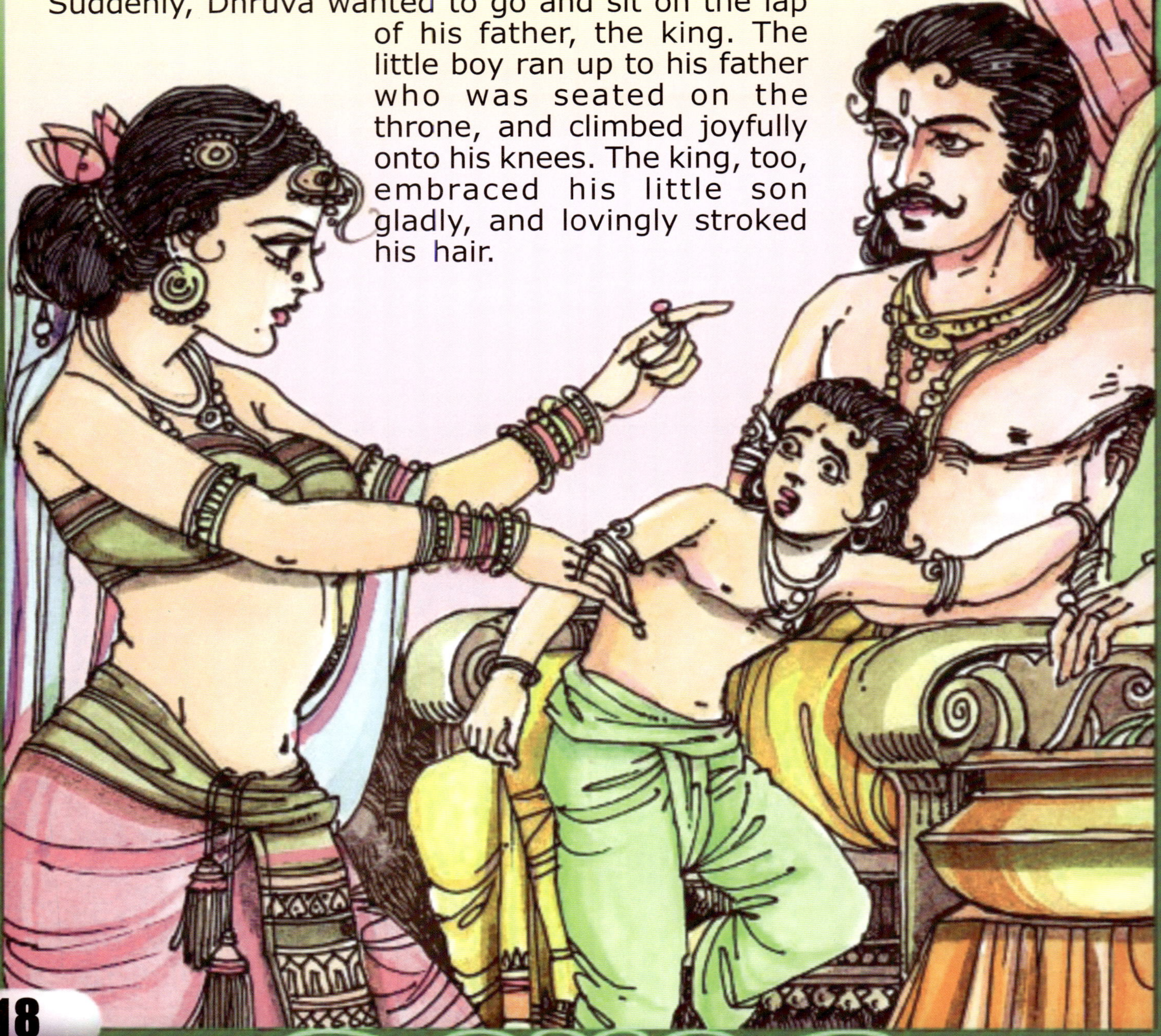

Queen Suruchi happened to come there, at that time. A proud and arrogant woman, she was incensed to see Dhruva on the king's knees. Rudely, she pulled the little boy by the ear and pushed him away.
"Get out from here!" she said to him in a rage. "You have no right to be seated here-on the lap of your father, or on his throne! That is a position meant for my son alone!"
The king, who was infatuated with his younger wife, said not a word in defence of his son.
Dhruva ran to his mother. "How is it that my father's lap is not for me?" he questioned her in anguish. "Tell me how I may obtain his love, so that no one can push me away from my rightful place. "Suniti was a pious and devoted woman, and a loving mother. She said to her son, "My dear child, look not to your earthly father and earthly mother for comfort. Turn instead, to your Divine Father. He has the power to grant you your heart's desire."

Dhruva's heart was touched with his mother's words of wisdom. He went into the tapoban-the forest of meditation-in order to find God, through the practice of austerity and devotion. Maharishi Narad came to meet him there. From the sage, Dhruva received the taraka-mantra that would enable him to have a darshana of the Lord, "Om Namo Bhagavate Vasudevaya!" (I offer salutations to the Lord who is the All-Pervading One!)

For days together, this five-year-old child sat in meditation upon the Lord. Hunger, thirst and all bodily demands were put aside. As he uttered the taraka-mantra repeatedly, his consciousness was uplifted, and the Lord appeared to give him darshana.

Dhruva had left the palace with the longing to regain his rightful place on his father's throne and in his heart. But the Lord's darshan wrought a tremendous transformation into his soul. The constant repetition of the mantra had kindled his highest aspirations. With folded hands and bowed head, Dhruva said to the Lord, "I want neither the reins of power, nor the pleasures of this earth, I want Thee and Thee alone!" The Lord so blessed Dhruva that he was transformed into a most steadfast star on the horizon-the Pole Star. The boy, who had been pushed away from his father's knee, became the Beloved of the Lord. As the Pole Star, the Dhruva-Nakshatra, he shines on; steadily, not moving from his place,
come summer or winter!

PRIDE GOES BEFORE A FALL

There was a king who had everything a man could ask for-health, wealth, pleasures and power. He was the mighty ruler of a vast kingdom, and was proud of it. One day, a holy man came to him and said, "O King, you should not be proud of your strength, your possessions and your power, for they are transient. Either you will leave them one day, or they will leave you."

The king could not understand this. He flew into a rage. But the holy man persisted, "O King, learn to be humble. In the measure in which you become humble, in that measure you will become a channel of God's forces for the healing of suffering mankind."

Infuriated, the pompous king thundered, "Why must I be humble? I have such a vast kingdom. I have just to lift my finger and thousands of people will come to do my bidding. Why must I be humble? I do not need your advice. I order you to leave right away!"

A few days later, the king went out hunting, with his ministers

and courtiers. Seeing a magnificent deer at a distance, he chased it. Soon he was separated from the rest of his retinue. The elusive deer seemed to have disappeared into thin air. Unwilling to give up the pursuit, the king spurred on his horse to gallop faster and faster. Suddenly, he caught a glimpse of the deer, before it disappeared yet again. Egged on by the sight, the king tried to ride faster. Just as his horse took a giant leap forward, it stumbled and fell. Both horse and rider crashed to the ground, unconscious.

There they lay, levelled to the ground, until a few dacoits happened to pass by. Finding the horse and the rich rider in an unconscious state, they looted the king of his possessions, his weapons and stripped him naked. When the king regained consciousness, he was shocked at what he saw. In that helpless condition, he remembered the words of the holy man; they seemed to ring in his ears, "These things will either leave you or you will leave them, one day."

The king was overcome with remorse. He realised that it was his pride that had brought him to this predicament. He closed his eyes and offered a simple prayer, "In this state of utter helplessness, Lord, I turn to Thee! Do Thou help me. Else, here, in this dark jungle, the animals will soon devour me!"

Just then, he heard the roar of a lion. His heart trembled. However, he found that the lion's roar had stirred the horse awake. Grateful with relief, he mounted the horse and galloped across the valley to where his ministers and friends were anxiously searching for him.

From then on, the king's life was transformed. He became a man of humility. Every night, he reminded himself of the great teaching, "O man, be not proud of your possessions and power. They are fickle as the shifting sands of a desert."

THE STORY OF THE AMARPHAL

Raja Bharatrahari was a great man in every sense of that term. He was a just and merciful king. He was good to everyone. Verily, he was a model king.

One day, they brought to him an amarphal-the fruit of immortality-and said to him, "O king, this fruit is the only one of its kind. We have brought it to you because you are the one person who deserves to live for ever and ever more."

Bharatrahari accepted the fruit. But as he was about to

eat it, he said to himself, "Of what use is life to me without my beloved? Let me give this amarphal to my wife, whom I love more than my life. Let her live for ever and ever more."

So the king passed the amarphal to his wife saying, "This is the fruit of immortality, eat it and you, my beloved, will never die."

The queen accepted the fruit. But as destiny would have it, she was secretly in love with the coachman. She said to herself, "Of what use will this fruit be to me if I live on, but my dear coachman perishes?" So she passed on the fruit to the coachman.

As for the coachman, he was in love with a prostitute. He handed over the fruit to the prostitute.

In a moment of rare introspection, the prostitute said to herself, "Of what use is life to me? The longer I live, the more sins I commit and the more I drag other people into a life of sinfulness. If there is anyone who deserves to live eternally, it is our great and good and just king, Raja Bharatrahari."So back came the

amarphal to Raja Bharatrahari.
The king was amazed, he was dumbfounded! How did this fruit get into the hands of this prostitute? He made enquiries. He found that his wife had been faithless to him. "What a fool I was to have placed my trust in the world and in a creature of this world!" he said to himself. "Let me lay all my trust in Him who never faileth. Let me set out in quest of the One and only One Beloved, the First and the Only Fair, the Purest of the Pure, the Spotless, the Stainless."
His life was changed. He was born anew. Renouncing his kingdom, he became a jignasu, a seeker of Truth.

I AM NOTHING

A young man inherited a great fortune on his father's passing away. The lure of gold, however, meant little to him. His heart was fired with the love of God. He set out in search of a Guru who could lead him out of untruth into Truth, out of death into the Life Undying. He learnt of a teacher of spiritual wisdom. The teacher had an ashrama, and whosoever joined it had to first dedicate all his property and possessions to the ashrama.

Accordingly, the young man sold all he had and offered it to the Guru who, then, passed on to him the secret which was supposed to make him emancipated and free!

What was the secret? The young man

was asked to affirm, again and again, *"Aham Brahmasmi!* I am Brahman! I am God! I am the Supreme!"
The young man did so with all the sincerity and faith of which he was capable.
"I am God! I am Supreme!" he repeated to himself, again and again.
"Aham Brahmasmi! I am God!"
The words were uttered with every beat of his heart.
What was the result? Far from being emancipated and free, the young man's condition grew more and more miserable. He felt distressed in mind. He felt unhappy.
In due course, he fell ill. He could no longer stay at the ashrama. Penniless, having given away all he had to the Guru, he came out of the ashrama and, as good fortune would have it, came in contact with another teacher.
He advised the young seeker to give up saying, "I am God!" and to affirm instead, "I am nothing!"
This the young man did, and it was not long before he became sound in body, mind and spirit!

A MEANING IN EVERYTHING

Long ago, a sister, came to me. Her eyes were touched with tears. She sobbed as she spoke. Her husband, whom she loved and who loved her, had decided to travel to a distant land for purposes of business. He did not lack money.
God had given them much more than they needed.
"He does not need to go so far, leaving me here all alone," she said. "Pray that he may abandon this idea altogether."
My answer might have appeared cruel to her, at that time.
"I do not pray for this or that to happen," I said to her. "I shall pray that you may grow into understanding of what God wills for you and that you may cooperate with His Will and let It work, uninterrupted, in and through you!"
The day arrived when she bade her husband a tearful goodbye. "You did not do anything for me," she said to me. "You could have helped me

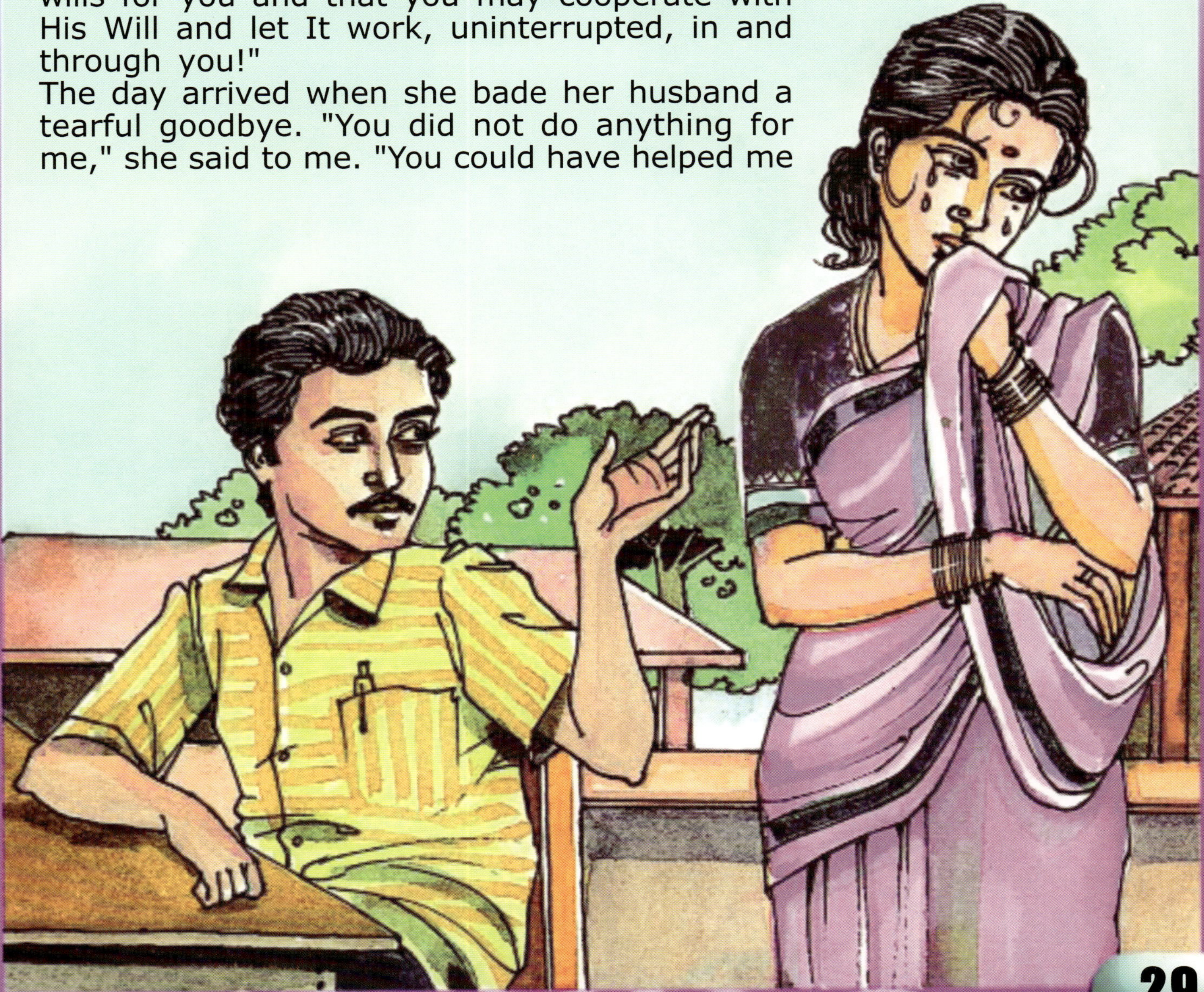

if only you had wished to do so!"
I smiled and said to her, "Sister! Do not despair! God fulfils Himself in many ways!"

After a few months, she met me again. Her face was wreathed in smiles. She was full of the joy of a child.
"Now I know," she said, "that there is the Hand of Divine Love and Wisdom in all that happens.
When my husband left, I wept and wept. Then, gradually, it dawned on me that if God had willed my dear one to travel to a far country, it must also be for my good. Indeed, it has proved to be so. My husband's going away has given me many spare hours. I utilise them in the study of the Gita and the Guru Granth Sahib and Sadhu Vaswani's books on the Sant-bani and the lives of saints. I pray and meditate. I sit in Sadhu Vaswani's holy company. I sing God's Name and I serve the children of the poor and the lowly. They love me and I love them. And I feel happy and blest!"

IS NOT GOD OUR FATHER

Birbal was much beloved of Emperor Akbar; he wasAkbar's favourite minister-an uncommon man of soundcommon sense. Many were the scintillating conversationsthe two had together; time seemed to fly when Akbar was inhis company.

One day, Akbar said to Birbal, "I marvel at some of the fantastic beliefs that you Hindus hold. You believe that the Lord comes to this earth in the garb of a human being- what an absurd notion this is!"

"What is so absurd about it, sire?" asked Birbal. "The Creator of the cosmos is also the Father of us all. Is it so fantastic that a father should come down to earth to save

his children?"
"Of course it is fantastic and absurd," Akbar insisted. "Why should the Creator of the cosmos soil his Divine Form and plunge into the *sansar sagar*- the ocean of existence?"
Birbal made no reply.
A few days passed. Emperor and Minister were taking a leisurely stroll along the banks of the Yamuna. On the river was sailing a pleasure-boat; the Emperor's infant-son sat on the knees of his nurse, and was enjoying his leisurely boatride. When the nurse saw Akbar and Birbal on the bank of the river, she was so startled, that she tried to stand up in the boat-and the child on her knees fell into the waters!

Emperor Akbar was astounded! Without a moment's hesitation, he plunged into the cold waters of the river to save his son. Swimming fast, he reached the floating child- only to realize that it was but a doll that had been thrown into the waters!
Birbal swam after the king to meet him in mid-river. "Even as an earthly father, sire, you plunged into the waters, and did not in the least bother about your royal robes getting soiled," he said to Akbar. "Does not our Heavenly Father love us a million times more than we love our children? Would he not plunge into the murky waters of the sansar-sagar to save His children?"
The Emperor made no attempt to answer his Minister.

THE ROBBER BECOMES A SAINT

"Stand still, O hermit! Stand still!"It was a terrible voice that uttered these words; the voice of a bandit whose very name struck terror in the hearts of those who heard his name-Angulimala.

Angulimala-"garland of thumbs"-was a fierce bandit who had plundered, looted and killed ruthlessly. His name had been acquired from the horrific practice of

chopping off the thumbs of his victims and stringing them as a garland around his neck, as a trophy of his bloody deeds.
Now, with a flashing sword in his hand and murder in his heart, the dreaded bandit chased the Buddha. He ran as fast as he could, but the Buddha eluded him.
Vexed and frustrated, Angulimala cried out from a distance, "Stand still, O hermit! Stand still!"
Quick came the simple, significant answer of the Buddha, "I am still! May you be still!"
When the bandit confronted him, the Blessed One explained to Angulimala what it was to stand still. The words of the Master went deep into the heart of the robber and he was converted. The bandit became a disciple and his heart, in due course, became tranquil as the surface of a lake on a clear, windless day.
To enter into the Peace of God is to relax and stand still-to stand where you are.

MY DOOR IS ALWAYS OPEN FOR YOU

A young girl had strayed from the path of virtue. She had broken the hearts of her pious, loving parents and left home to pursue a life of sinful pleasure.

Now she was ruined! Alone, abject and friendless, she felt she was lost beyond redemption. The only thing that she could do was to end her own life. But even as she contemplated suicide, she was impelled by

a strong urge to visit her childhood home, just once, for the very last time in her life.
She chose a dark night to return home, hoping that she might come away from there, unseen by anyone.
To her shock, she found the door of the humble cottage wide open, even in the middle of the night.
Fearing the worst, she called out impulsively, "Mother, are you all right?"
In an instant, her old mother stood in the open doorway. "Welcome home my child," she called. "We knew you would come back to us one day!"
The girl fell at her mother's feet, sobbing uncontrollably.
"Ah mother!" she wept, "I don't deserve your love!" "It is long since you left us my dear," said the mother. "But we have continued to pray for you day and night. 'Bring her home safely, my Lord!' We have asked Him again and again. Whether you came by night or by day, we wanted you to see the ever open door of your home, and know that you are always welcome here!"
God is like our Mother. He is always waiting to receive us, in love and forgiveness. Let us return to our true Home.

TUKARAM'S COMPASSIONATE HEART

Tukaram was that rare being-an honest and sincere grocer, who always sold good quality stuff at very reasonable prices. As such, he was a popular shopkeeper in the village of Dehu where he lived. Tukaram's one weakness-if we can call it such-was his tender and compassionate heart. The villagers took full advantage of his good nature. Not a day passed, without someone or the other coming to him with a long story of misfortune and sorrow. Tukaram listened to them, and his heart melted. He lent them money, which they seldom bothered to return. Yet others took away goods from his shop on credit-exploited his generosity to such an extent that the shop eventually had to be closed down.

Deeply concerned by the failure of her husband's business, Tukaram's wife sold her jewels to raise

money. Prudently, she urged her husband to start his business afresh- not in their own village, where his good nature had become a liability, and people bullied him effortlessly, but in a neighbouring village, where no one knew him, and his weakness would not be exploited.

Her advice proved to be sound. Tukaram took to selling salt in his new business effort, and succeeded in making a tidy sum-more than he had ever earned before! Happily Tukaram decided to return home.

On the way, he encountered a crowd of people, who had surrounded a poor man and were thrashing him soundly. The man wept and wailed in pain, but his attackers showed no mercy on him.Tukaram's heart melted at the sight; he intervened to rescue the poor man.

"Why do you beat up this defenceless man?" he enquired.

"Who? This rascal? Don't you pity this defenceless man," sneered his tormentors." He has borrowed money left and right, and not returned a single paisa. We are his creditors, and we are determined to teach the rogue a lesson he will never forget."

"How much money does he owe you?" asked Tukaram as usual, his compassion getting the better of his prudence.

The creditors mentioned the amount. Tukaram counted the money he was carrying; he had more than they were asking for. Immediately, the debt was paid, and Tukaram accompanied the poor man to his house. A sad sight met his eyes at the house of the stranger. The family was in a truly pitiable condition; his starving children were crying for food.

Tukaram's tender heart was so moved that he gave to the poor man the little money that remained with him. He then returned to his village, empty-handed!

His wife was furious. Her precious jewels, and her careful plans had all been thrown away by the foolish compassion of her husband!

She dragged him to the village panchayat and complained bitterly to the village elders. They found that her grievances were quite justified. They pronounced Tukaram to be an utter fool. A garland of onions was thrown round his neck, and he was paraded through the village on a donkey's back as the most stupid man in the entire village. Those very people, who had exploited him and borrowed money from him, now ridiculed and scorned him.

What is folly in the eyes of selfish men, is much beloved of the Lord! The same Tukaram later became the singing saint, whose abhangas have become immortal. Thousands revere him today, along with Mira and Surdas, as one intoxicated with the love of the Lord.

WONDROUS ARE THE WAYS OF GOD

King Fredrick the Great was about to drink his cup of chocolate when he remembered that he had not read from the pages of the scripture as he usually did before taking breakfast.

While he read the morning thought, a spider wove its net over his cup. When he came back and saw the cobweb, the king asked for a fresh cup of chocolate.

His servant carried the untouched cup into the kitchen. One of the cooks, pale with fright, asked in a

tremulous voice, "Didn't the king want his cup of chocolate?"
"No", answered the servant. "The king has asked for a fresh cup."
"Then, I am ruined!" exclaimed the cook. He took out a revolver and shot himself.
The astonished servant spilt a little of the chocolate on the floor. A dog came and licked it and died on the spot, in convulsions.
Apparently, the chocolate had been poisoned by the cook who shot himself because he thought he had been exposed.

WHERE DO YOU SEEK ME ?

There was a cobbler who was a true devotee of God. As he went about his daily work, repairing and mending shoes, his eyes would rain tears, "O God! When will I have a vision of Thy beauteous Face?"

Again and again, this aspiration awoke within his heart. His heart was full of love and longing for the Lord.

"O God! When shall I have a vision of Thy beauteous Face?"

One day, he heard a Voice say to him, "My child! Tomorrow, early in the morning, go out into yonder streets. I shall come and meet thee!"

He was anxious for the next morning to break. Very early in the morning, he went out into the street. There he found a woman with a

child in her arms, both covered in bare rags and shivering in the intense cold of the wintry morning.
He approached the woman and said to her, "Why are you out here in the cold of the winter?"
The woman said to him, "I am homeless. I have no house and the whole night, I have sat here and shivered. My limbs have become numb with cold and my child is almost frozen to death. We have not had a morsel for a whole day!"
"Come with me," said the cobbler.
Bringing them into his house, he gave them clothes and blankets. And then he prepared a bed for them.
He said to the woman, "Lie down and rest for a while. I shall go and prepare food for you. Take that food and rest for a while, for you are in need of rest."

As he gave them clothes, as he gave them blankets, as he prepared a bed for them, he found the face of the woman lit by a radiant smile. Looking at that smile, the cobbler said to himself, "This, indeed, is a vision of the Face of God!"

THE VALUE OF A SINGLE BREATH

Alexander, the great, was on his death-bed. After fighting many battles, he was on his way home when, suddenly, he caught fever and could not travel further.

He was surrounded by anxious physicians as well as the ministers of his empire and the commanders of his army. Turning to them, he said, "I have a longing to see my mother and seek her blessings before I die. Is there anyone here who will give me a few healthy days of his life, so that I can reach home and have one last glimpse of my sweet mother? In exchange, I will give him one half of my kingdom!"

There was no answer.Even for half of Alexander's vast empire, there

was not a man present who could offer a few days of his precious life. Alexander's death was near. He felt he was about to die. Feebly he said, "Is there anyone who can give me but one breath of his life? I will give him my entire kingdom in exchange!"

There was no answer. Alexander died with the following words on his lips, "I wasted millions of my breaths to carve out a great empire. In exchange for that empire, I could not get a single breath of life!"

THE TEST OF FAITH

Milarepa, the great Tibetan Yogi, came to his Guru one day, and begged to be accepted as a disciple. "Master, my faith in you is beyond words," asserted Milarepa.

"What is the extent of your faith?" asked the Guru.

"It is as wide as the limitless skies," came the answer.

The Guru heard the words but wanted to put the disciple to a test.

"Here are some bricks," he said Milarepa. "Build a platform right here, with these."

Milarepa set to work immediately. He built a beautiful platform which he felt should please his Guru.

When the Guru arrived, he exclaimed, "What a fool you are, Milarepa! You have wasted all your time and energy. I did not want a platform here, at this corner, but at the other corner."

Milarepa thought, "I clearly remember the Guru pointing to this spot! But I shall not let my faith be shaken. I must be wrong. The Guru is always right!" He dismantled the platform and started building a new one at the other corner.

After a few days, the second platform was ready and Milarepa approached his Guru.

Once again, the Guru was dissatisfied and said, "What a careless fellow you are! I did not want the platform here!"
Milarepa was exasperated, but controlled himself and said, "Let me not doubt the Gurul" He built a third platform.
The process was repeated several times and now Milarepa could take it no longer. He lost his patience. His faith was completely shaken.He wanted to run away from the Guru.The Guru's wife senced it and came to his rescue.

The Guru is only testing you, she comforted him.It was you who told him that your faith was limitless as the skies.Where is your faith now? Milarepa's faith was renewed.He build yet another platform. When it was ready,the Guru embraced him,saying, "you are truely my own. Let me share with you the secret which I have shared with none else."
Milarepa sat at the feet of the Guru and received from him what only a Guru can pass on to his disciple.He was enlightened.

THROUGH THE FOREST OF LIFE

Jatila, a little boy, lived with his mother at the fringe of the forest in a broken cottage. His school was situated at the other end of the forest. Everyday he had to make his way through the forest. When he left at dawn and when he returned at dusk, he could hear the fearful sounds of animals. Sometimes he felt so helpless. Fright and terror overtook him almost everyday, as he crossed the forest. He spoke of this to his mother.

"My child Jatila, why must you worry?" the mother exclaimed. "Your elder brother lives in the forest, why don't you call out to him?"

Surprised, the child asked, "Elder brother? Who is he, what is his name? Where was he for so long? Why didn't you mention this to me earlier?"

"Your elder brother is named Krishna," said the mother. "Whenever

you feel frightened, whenever you need anything, call out to Him, He will come and appear in front of you. He will escort you to school."

The next day when Jatila reached the forest, he cried out, "Krishna, Krishna! Come to me and lead me out of this forest."

There was no answer. But out of the fullness of his heart, with faith and devotion, out of a heart that felt utterly helpless, Jatila cried out again, and again, "Krishna! Krishna! Come to me."

Seeing the faith and love of this child, Krishna appeared before him in the form of a young man and said to him, "Jatila, my brother, here am I!"

He held Jatila's hand and walked with him to his school and said, to him, "Jatila, never feel lonely! Whenever you need Me, just call out to Me. I shall come and be with you."

This life, too, is a forest. Temptations surround us, fears daunt us, difficulties and problems overpower us and we feel helpless, frightened, lonely. All we need to do is to call out to Krishna with faith and devotion, and He will appear before us.

TOLA'S TRANSFORMATION

A rich man was moving along the roadside one cold wintry night when he found a man sleeping on the pavement. The man was shivering because he had nothing to cover him. The wealthy man went up to him, looked into his face and recognised him as a son of his one time friend.

"Tola, what has happened to you?" he asked. "Why are you lying like this in the cold of the wintry night?"

"You know of my condition!" replied Tola. "I have gambled away all I had, I am totally penniless now."

Immediately the wealthy man got a blanket and with it he covered Tola.

A few days later, as the rich man happened to pass by the same road, he was surprised to find Tola sleeping without the blanket.
"Tola!" he exclaimed, "What have you done with the blanket?"
Tola said, "Sir! What can I do? I am a slave to gambling. I gambled; I lost; and to make good the loss, I had to sell the blankets."
For a second time, the rich man gave Tola a blanket, yet again the same thing happened. After a few days, Tola gambled and sold the blanket. This process was repeated twelve times in succession. Time and again, the rich man gave a blanket to Tola; and time and again, Tola gambled it away!
Even after the thirteenth time, the patience of this rich man
had not worn out. He had been given this teaching that howsoever low and sunken in sin a man may be, cloth and food must not be denied to him.
Undaunted, for the thirteenth time, he brought a blanket to cover the shivering body of Tola, in the cold of the wintry night. And now Tola's

conscience woke up.
He remonstrated with himself, "Shame upon you! Over and over again, this rich man gave a blanket to you and each time you went and sold it! But the rich man's patience is boundless. Shame upon you!"
With this realisation came a transformation in the life of Tola. He resolved never to gamble again. By the grace of God, he turned over a new leaf.

Other books for Children
by
J.P. Vaswani

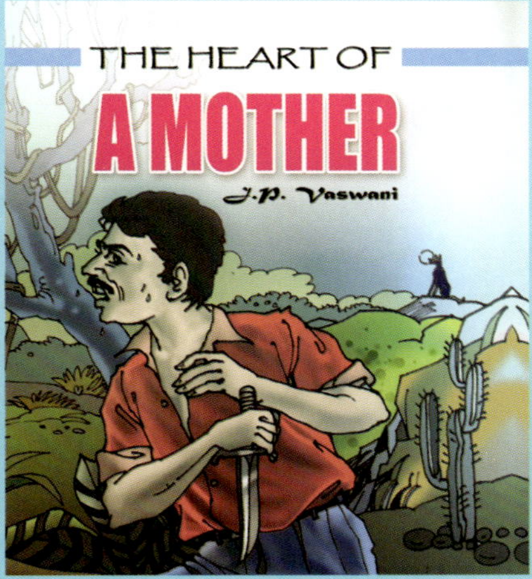

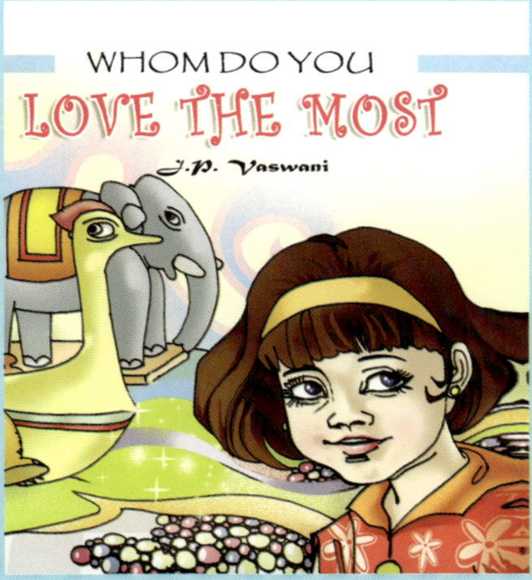

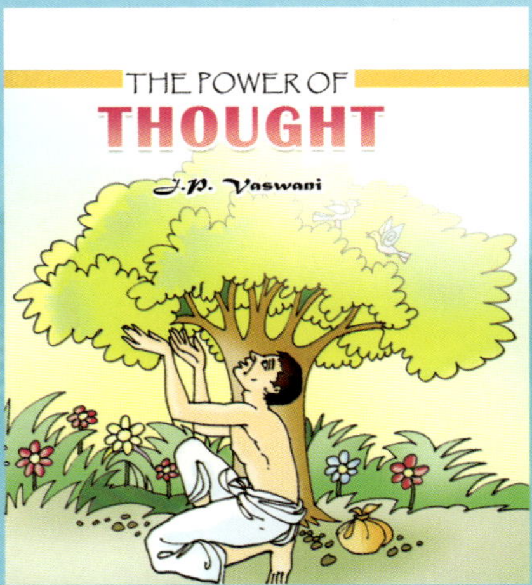

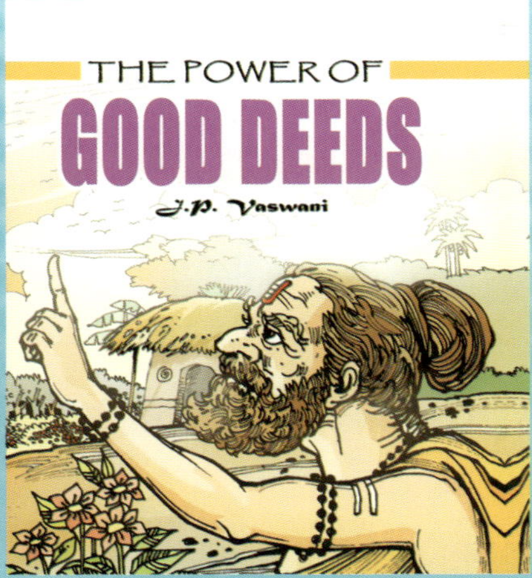

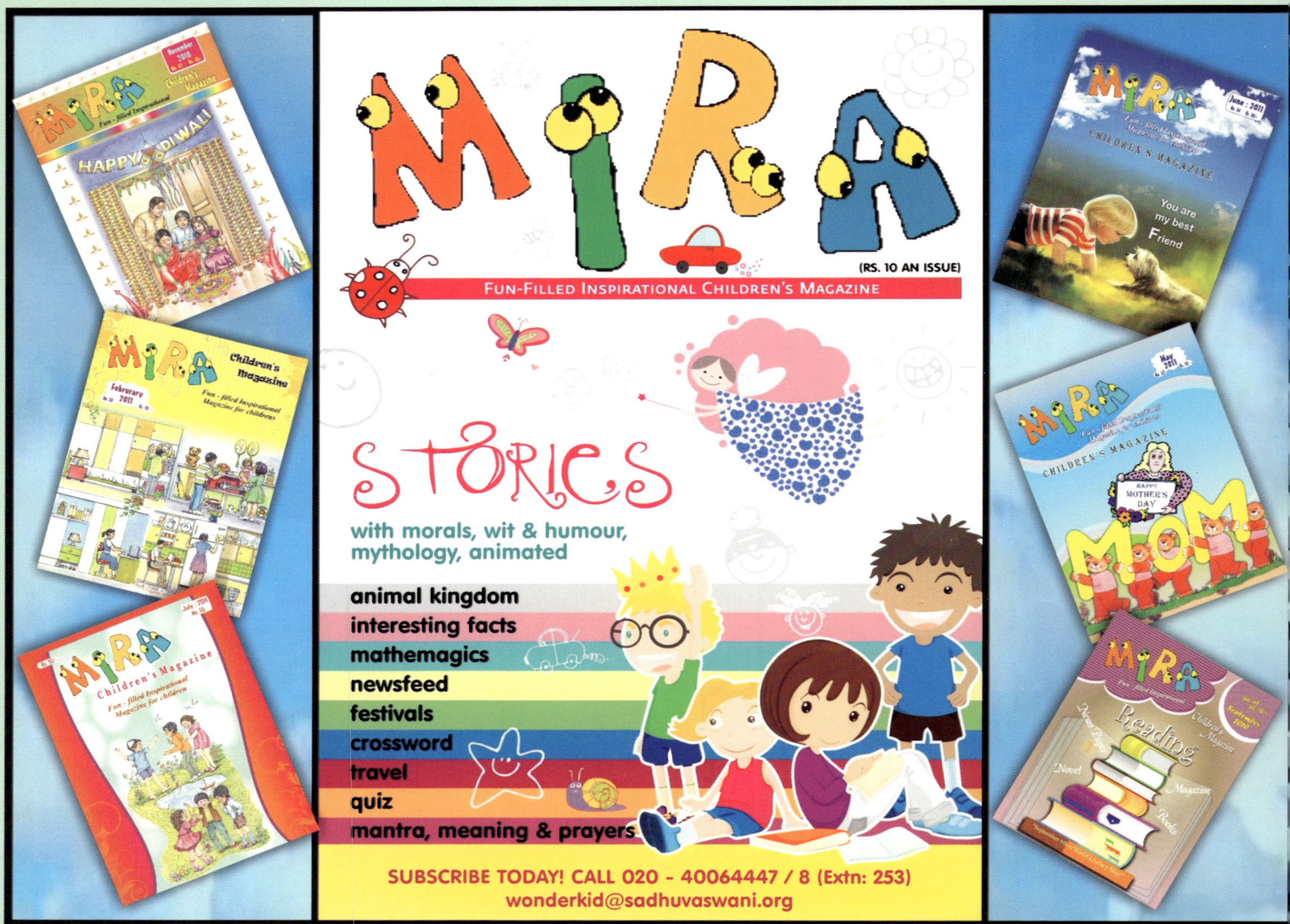

Subscribe Now

* **MIRA** - **Fun Filled, Inspirational Children's Monthly Magazine** *

An exciting journey of discovery to empower your child and help him realise his true potential!

Please fill in BLOCK letters

Name :______________________________

Age :________________

Address :______________________________

____

____

Pin code :______________________________

Tel:__________________________________

Mobile :______________________________

E - mail :______________________________

Subscription for
1 year INR. 100/- US$ 25
2 years INR. 190/- US$ 45
3 years INR. 280/-US$ 65

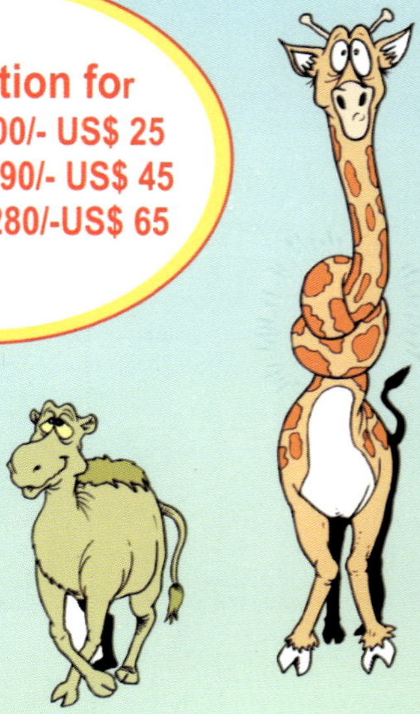

SEND IN YOUR SUBSCRIPTIONS TO

THE EDITOR

MIRA

Sadhu Vaswani Mission, 10, Sadhu Vaswani Path, Pune - 411 001.

Tel. : +91-20-40064447 / 8 Email : wonderkid@sadhuvaswani.org

Subscriptions may be sent by Cash or D. D. payable to SADHU VASWANI MISSION, Pune.